Thank you for your time.

Thank you for your time.

the inside of my notes|

Intro:

Speak me out loud.
Speak me throughout your soul.

Welcome to the journey,

of a hummingbird.

you came back and told me
how great your life is without me.
whats the purpose, when you already left?
but i stayed and listened.
hoping youd tell me
you missed me,
as much i missed you.

you came back and told me about him.
the boy you replaced me with.
oh how bad it hurt to listen,
but i still did.
hoping youd see my loyalty,
see how much im going through
to show you my love for you.

you came back and told me about
everything thats happening in your life.
your problems, your relationship problems.
i stayed and listened.
i stayed and gave you advice.
i stayed!
even if staying made me look hopelessly a fool.
even when i hated myself for staying.
even when i ruin every relationship for staying.
even when i hated myself for loving you.
i stayed.
hoping youd see these problems were useless,
because im the one youre searching for.

you asked if we could be friends.
oh how bad it hurt to hear that,
but i tried.
if it means id have you in my life.
hoping youd see me trying,

hoping somehow it would change your mind.

after a while,
i realized you were using my outlet as a recharge.
using me.
and i let you.
hoping you might come more often.
hoping youd tell me you fell in love with me again.
like i did with you.
but you never did.

i kept hoping.

hoping for the person i fell in love with.
but my hope for the person that was already gone
was destroying me.
you were destroying love for me.
isnt this what everyone wants,
unwavering loyalty?
unconditional love?
why cant i be what you need?

throughout this time i realized i cant blame you,
when i allowed you to hurt me.

i just thought it wouldve ended up differently.

How you could replace us like we were nothing.

How could you move on so effortlessly,
making me feel crazy for still loving you.

How could you easily replace us,
making me second guess myself.
Questioning,
if I was ever enough in the first place.

How could you move on so effortlessly
when you said,
I'm the one you want to spend the rest of your life with.
Did that mean nothing?
Did all our history mean nothing?

How could you easily replace us,
when i'm still mourning you.

They revealed that there's an end to loving me.
That i'll forever be a placeholder
until your true love comes.
I was a good show and tell
until I wasn't.

- I am replaceable

but just for a second,
i wanna forget everything.
and spend one last night,
with you.

-we owe us a better ending.

Why am I still defending you

to myself?

What's wrong with me that makes you leave me
over and over again.
What do I have to change to make you stay?
Pick me apart, choose the features you want.
Taller?
Funnier?
Prettier?
Talkative?
Happier?
Different gender?

Change me until I am your favorite version of myself.
Change me until i'm enough for you.

questioning myself to the point,
that i finally understand
how you moved on so quickly.

i wouldnt even be enough for myself.

-degrading

They said take it,

it will finally make you happy

as they shove the green pills down my throat.

Years later...

I stare at the bottle in my hand

and they whisper,

"I am the only reason

you're happy."

- antidepressants

A note to you:

I wished you came at a different time.
I can't love you the way you deserve
right now.

Will you wait for me?

realizing why they left me,
by being in a relationship with myself.

the action of putting other peoples opinions on yourself.
letting them take control of your hand
as the metal rectangle shows the scarlet red
embedded in your thighs.
creating scars.
scars of forgetting your worth, your value.
scars embedded by your own hands.

A note to you:

As you speak, I sit and analyze every syllable you pronounce.
Seeing the judgment you speak against others
that are your past.
I wonder if you do that against me.
Spit my name and put your judgment.
Judging the way I healed from what we broke.
My love, stop looking at me or your once was.
You need to see you're putting so much time into people
that aren't even there.
That your time is too short, too precious to be wasting it on the
past, on the negative.
You should be looking at you.
You need to stop looking in the past,
because you could be a beautiful hummingbird
if you choose to heal.

The one night stand that met
all your emotional and spiritual
needs.

- drained

July 18, 2021 at 22:33

im up,
thinking of you.
checking my phone repeatedly.
even though i havent received any notifications.
hoping somehow, i missed it.
but how could i.
i have a feeling you might text me on my birthday, its a week from
now. its funny to think ive never celebrated one with you, even
though we have known each other for years. its weird to think every
time my day comes around you arent here.

but if you do text me on my day, it wont mean as much to me. its
the only excuse for you to text me and leave me again.
i wanna hear from you on a normal day. on a day that has no
special meaning behind it. where i can actually feel every word you
type. so please don't text me, to say two little words just for you to
leave me again. show me i mean more to you than i think you do.

that's why i am up.
thinking of you.
waiting for your notification.

waiting for you.

How could I ever
love someone else
purely, innocently,
unconditionally,
after you tainted my love.

Attention

do i have to cut my wrist
as you watch them bleed,
for you to notice me?

and after a while
i started to change myself,
for you.

- my story in eleven words

Why can't I ever love you right?
you deserve better than me.

- loving myself

I tried to make a song out of you,
but it didn't capture your beauty.
Writing you out like this,
I can feel you throughout my body.
Like you're the blood running through my veins.
This is your truest form.
Where you're the most beautiful.

"You're beautiful," you said sincerely.

Like it's the most genuine honesty you've ever told.

It pains me to know that
my love wasn't enough.

Could you accept me for my gender?
When my mother said " Men will always give them what girls don't have."
She told me I would never be enough for girls like you.

Could you accept me for not having money?
When there are other people that can give your dream experience.

Could you accept me for my body?
When my binge eating changed everything you used to love.
I am not the body type you fall in love with on the internet.

Could you accept me after I tell you everything i've done?
How could you not run away?

Could you handle my depression?
Help comfort the way I feel?
Or am I too much work for too little reward?

Could you accept at times i'm silent,
or will you think i'm too boring?

Could you stay when I know i'll fall short.
Reassure me and tell me,
"you're worth more than you think of yourself."

Could you be patient,
because I know i'm damaged.
I know I need healing.
Would you heal with me?

Could you accept me?
Like. The real me?
Or am I too much to ask?

but every time i express how i feel
you punish me for it.

and you ask why im closed off

You have to start
to love yourself
the way you love
the toxic ones

am i doing the same things i did with you
with another person
to create you in my life again
to feel you again

-*im still looking for you in the midst of everyone, and everything.*

<3

you're the feeling i never knew i needed.

The cycle of being

in love,
falling out of love,
into,
falling in love,
with someone else.

I knew you weren't the one
but somehow, I fell deeply.
So deep into you.
That I tried to jam the pieces,
that are you and I,
to fit each other.
Knowing that we aren't right
for our own puzzle.

I can't come back to you,
I can't compare to what your life is without me.

How could I ever compete.
How will I ever be enough for you.

The metal rectangle
helped carve your initial into my arm.
So you'll always be with me,
even when you leave me.

-Tattoo twin

I wanna love myself the way I love you...

consistently

A note to you:

I'm giving my time to people that are undeserving of it.
Bending backwards, stopping everything to be with them.
But why aren't I like that with people that are worth my time?
That will respect me.
You aren't deserving of that.
Being treated like your time isn't valued.
I'm sorry for making you feel unvalued, unwanted.
The fog is clearing up,
i'm seeing you,
your time and how precious it is to have it.
I hope it isn't too late.

<3

My love for you grew differently.
We never ever touched skin against another
and still we fell into each other,
intimately.
As if my heart was supposed to
love, and learn from you.

How do you have the nerve to come back
and ask for any form of us.
When you're the one that left us, left me.
Because I would've loved you for lifetimes.
I would've given up my future for you.
I didn't want this, I didn't choose this, you did.
I deserve better than to have someone that will always leave me.
I deserve better than to have someone
who will never see my quality.
And now I know better than to allow you
to have my bleeding heart
in your hands,
again.

"Sun kiss me,
i'll show you my scars.
remind me of change
as you darken my skin.
lay me bare
and touch me
in places, no lover could.
smother me in your warmth.
show me what it's like to be loved by you."

I'm insecure to share my writings with my loved ones.
I don't wanna hear their judgment,
the good or the bad.
My writings are pure, untouched by any influence but my own.
And i'm scared if I shared them,
i'll lose my voice again.

we're all here for a set amount of time.
and i decided to waste some of my time,
with you.

-waste my time

<3

how could someone like you fancy me?

you're too beautiful to love me.

i can't play the victim
when it's my fault for allowing you
to think,
how you were treating me
was okay.

Why won't I allow myself to let go of my walls?
Why can't I allow anyone to love me?
Why do I allow the fear of being vulnerable control me?
Why do I still give you so much power over me?

I wanna open up to you.
I wanna be loved and cherished.
But is this person worth the risk?
Is what i'm feeling real?
Or am I over fantasizing?
Is this a waste of my time?
How do I know when to let go of my walls?
Universe, please send me a sign?

***Universe, please tell me what to do, because taking the risk
too much to ask myself.***

-at war with myself

A passing note:

Have faith that everything will come together.

Your love how
consuming,
conditional,
draining,
selfish,
was the best thing.
You, breaking my heart
was the most selfless gift you gave me.
In the process of you doing so,
I found me.
The person I thought was gone.
You showed me the little girl that was hanging on by a thread.
At that moment,
I decided to choose me.
So thank you,
for opening my eyes,
for the gift,
for breaking my heart.

All you can do is try.

–

Trying

<3

Never knew I could listen to someone
and fall in love with everything they say.
Every time you spoke,
you dissolved the rust that was built on top of me.
Showing parts of myself that I thought were gone.
You saw through my dandelion tinted glass,
and saw me.
The pure version of myself.
The version of myself I never knew, I could be.

- Never knew someone's love could be cleansing

Love me as if this limerence is never fading away.

A passing note:

Go on a morning walk.
Before the sun touches the horizon.
Go through nature and watch.
Watch the animals, how they live life unfazed of your presence.
Watch the way they live day by day, loving everything they can get.
Watch the people, the ones that run to gain self-love,
self-acceptance.
Watch the friends, the lovers. How they enjoy each other's
company before they head to their day.
Learn from them.
Go talk to yourself out loud. Learn every aspect of yourself.
Every thought, every feeling.
Get to know the person you're spending the rest of your life with.
Look for the beauty.
Because
In these moments is where you'll find the true meaning of
selflessness, love, life.
In these moments you'll find what it means to be alive.

i am afraid to love.
thinking everyones gonna love me,
the way you did.

Don't forget about the power
that lies between your thighs.

- getting yourself out there

A passing love note:

You're everything beautiful in the world.
Gorgeously complex.
Elegantly scripted in a way,
that even Aphrodite was star-struck.
The complete definition of unconditional.

A passing note:

Let go of the hidden figures you keep inside your closet for the rainy days. You were always doomed to fail once you put the figures in there. Let go, really, genuinely, let go. No matter how hard it is and how easy it is to hide the past, hide the figures that are comforting, unhealthy, and easy to fall back to. You need to move on because those figures are the reason you are there in the first place. I know how uncomfortable it is, how hard you're going to try, just to be knocked down. But every time it happens, you're gonna have to get yourself back up. Cleanse all influence that has been piling up, keep trying and never give up. Because you can't be living like this anymore. You deserve to be happy and healed. and Trust me, you are worth all your self-effort. Change your perspective and heal yourself. Let go, cause only then you'll find what you sought out for all this time.

I'm waiting on the day when
I look into someone's eyes,
and see my own love.

-Mutual

there is too much pain
to come back from.

are we even worth saving?

How perfectly you were written,
with no influence but raw emotions.
No figurative language to change your perspective.
Just you, *only you*.

The one that got away:

we arent strangers
but when it comes to love, we are.
friends that always wanted to be more.
and i know my insecurities are controlling the way we go.

but im wondering
if we're running out of time to be in love.
for me to be your first girl.
is it a phase or do you really love me?
because I dont wanna be another experiment.
i dont want to break up just for you to say, i wasnt your type.

but deep in my soul, i hope what we have here is true.
i hope we could fall in love together,
because i wanna learn from you.
i want you to teach me all the lessons
youve learned, and are learning.
as i do the same.
teach me, you.
and how you became the person you are today.
teach me how you need and want to be loved.
and ill do the same.
teach me your love.
as i do the same.

i hope that what we have here is true,
because all i wanna do in my lifetime,
is learn you.

- reciprocation

I'm still in love with the version of you that I created.

No one talks about how draining loving yourself becomes. How once you find yourself, the fear of losing yourself is overwhelming. That you rather not give any part of you to another person, or allow anyone to take down the walls you built.

Knowing when you do open up and get hurt, you'll blame yourself. Because you allowed them to get close to you. You allowed them to hurt you. So you consciously stay in your bubble. Thinking if there's only you in it, you'll never lose yourself to anyone again. But this cycle of trying to take the risk then choosing yourself has become lonely and toxic. Maybe taking the risk of getting hurt is the point of growing. But then again, taking the risk of getting hurt, is taking the risk of losing yourself. And why would you do that? If you worked so hard to find and build you.

-Is it possible you could lose yourself by yourself?

A passing note:

In the uncomfortable places is where you'll grow.

Already lived what could have been in my head.

- Anticipatory nostalgia

my heart and my sober self

been intoxicated by you for way too long,

i need a detox.

I put my fingers down my throat
to get rid of the products of
when I over-indulge with you

- binge eating

The sad part is, I know you love me.
But how you love, the way you love.
Isn't how or the way I want to be loved.
Being loved by you is draining and, exhausting at times.
And being loved by someone, loving someone,
shouldn't feel like that.

-Sometimes love isn't enough.

A passing love note:

Grow into your name.

<3

Suddenly then,
I forgot how much I missed you.

To the little girl inside of me.
I'll forever protect you.
I'll forever strive to honor you.
I might fail.
I might break our promises.
But I promise,
I'll find my way back to you.

I am meant for something great in life.
Maybe it's my sun in Leo talking.
Or maybe it's my Scorpio moon,
and how beautifully you can write your emotions.

For the first time, I smiled.
Laughed so deep,
my stomach joined in.
For the first time, I was happy.
And it wasn't because of you.

<3

in the midst of all my darkness,
there was you.
the most welcoming moonlight ive ever seen.

– god, i wished you could see yourself through my mind.

A passing note:

My relationship with food is helping me
with my other relationships.

"Even though it's comforting, doesn't mean it's the healthiest."

The idea of someone genuinely loving me more than I do towards them, is disgusting to me.
I've always been second place. People always chose others over me.
The act of you consciously, picking, choosing me, doesn't make sense.
When my ex lovers showed me that I could never be anyone's first choice.
That my love isn't worthy enough to stay and fight for it.
I know it ruins potential relationships because I don't believe them when they say, i'm worthy to be loved.
I've been corrupted in my mind to think that I have nothing to give, no worth behind myself.
That my love doesn't have any quality or uniqueness, enough for someone to actually love my love.
An unrequited love is all i've ever received.
So it doesn't make sense that you could genuinely love me,
because i've never been shown that type of love.
my type of love.

<3

My heart was getting prepared to find your love, your heart, your loyalty.
All the heartbreak before you was the universe telling me,
it wasn't our time yet.
To wait patiently to fully understand and appreciate everything you are.
The universe always knew my heart was meant to be,
unconditionally yours.
And now I know it's our time,
because everything with you feels meant to be.
All the love songs fit perfectly.

- You were worth the wait

<3

All the fears go away. All the walls drop.
Even the wall put against myself.
At this moment, i'm freely exposed.
With you, my secrets, my feelings
that I can't even admit to myself,
pour out.
With you, I pour, admit, purge, and cleanse.
With you, I see myself in a different lens.

-You love me the way i've always wanted to love myself.

My Prayer

Whoever is listening.
Whoever I have to believe in.
Universe?
God?

Please help me find my way.

I beg you...

I'm finally okay that you're in love with someone else.

<3

I've fallen in love before,
I know the pain, the hurt, the dissociation that comes with it.
But for the first time, you made me want to fall in love again.
Consciously knowing how my first went.
You made the consequences worth it,
if it means I could love you and, be loved by you.
So I'm walking into you,
knowing the consequences of falling in love.
Because you make love, beautiful again.

- You'll forever be engraved in my soul.

Is this love?

Allowing someone to show you that your love is gorgeous.
Enough for them to stay,
and learn every aspect of your love,
every form you come in.

The one that got away:

If I had one last moment with you.
I would tell you that it wasn't all in your head.
I would tell you that it wasn't a surface-level love.
I would tell you that you weren't the only one that felt it.
I would tell you that this was deep.
A love that keeps you up at night, hoping.
I would tell you that your love is once out of a lifetime.
A, can't breathe without you type of love.
I would tell you that your love was the realist love,
i've ever received.
A love that leaves after-effects.
A love I know, i'll never recover from.
I would tell you to kiss me now,
to remind each other,
how we're meant to be.

The most painful feeling is knowing you ruined a good thing, and knowing the person won't come back this time.

A passing note:

Don't assume how people feel,

you're taking their voice.

<3

I always thought I knew what love was,
until I met you.

-you give love a whole different meaning

<3

Everything I love about myself
is what you showed me

Our potential of what
we could've been,
tears me apart.

-our what ifs,
kills me inside.

Pandora's box

For our last act of love.
Let's put each other in this box.
Appreciate the love, the pain, the laughs,
the beautiful disaster we call us.
Appreciate that there's something about us
that no soul could ever take.
A flame that will never lose it's rage.
Our passionate fire we'll forever admire from a distance.

And then together,
Let us close each other in this box
and let go.
Because we're most beautiful,
closed.

we always knew
it would come to an end.
but why? why did we do it?
fall into one another
with your heart.
with your sanity.
with your every little thing.
knowing that there's an end.

– is this what it means to be human?

it's not ironic
that i started to fall for you,
when you decided
this wasn't worth it anymore.

it wouldn't be us,
if we didn't have
bad timing.

A passing note:

Patience
Discipline
Consistency

<3

The version of myself that i'm growing into,
is meant to be with you.

Advice:

Q:

A: Whatever you can live with.

Why do I feel enough for myself,
but inadequate for everyone else?

I crave validation.
Letting others
dictate my quality.

This isn't an everyday "teenage feeling,"
This isn't a situational or a temporary feeling.
This is my disease, my illness,
my luck of the draw.

This never-ending war between my self-love and depression.
This war, this fight, is the most exhausting and lonely you'll ever feel.

Sometimes, depression wins the battle.
At other times, my self-love achieves victory.
But i'm so scared of who's going to win in the end.

Because deep down
I know,
it will never be me,
and my self-love.

ill forever have to
beg someone
to see me

<3

you're the euphoria
after screaming at the top of your lungs
to a song
that explains the feelings
you thought
you were the only one that felt

- someone finally understands me

Chronological order

You called me to apologize. And I started to fall.

You would describe love the same way I do.
"Imma sucker for love too."

I admire the way you confidently know your worth. That you stand up for yourself even when it hurts. I admire and fell in love with the way you love yourself. I fell in love with everything that made you a better person.

The day we saw each other. The way you hugged me took me back to 8th grade. The way we looked at each other like we are in 6th period. The feeling of you, the butterflies, the nervousness. Throughout these years, I thought it would've faded away. But I still have never met anyone that came close to the way you feel. Isn't it your love they talk about in the movies? in songs? The one you can't really get over. Maybe the book you gave me was a perfect symbol of us. That it was us written in those pages.

And even though you aren't here.
I still have the book you gave me on that day.
It's in the back of my front seat.
And from time to time I hold it,
when missing you starts to hurt.

A passing note:

Happiness is in your perspective.

The one that got away:

I relive the conversations we never had. Talking to myself out loud as if you were there. Going on walks to tell each other about our day. I'll smile at those funny remarks you say. Going on drives to relive our unfinished plans. We sit amongst the moonlight and watch the stars dance. You'll show me the stars that make up the constellation of your heart, as I tell you i'll make sure they don't dirft apart. Right then and there, it's just us two. A love that's in a different hue.

(over fantasizing)

I love it when I numb myself with food,
I don't have to feel anymore.

I love it when I numb myself with alcohol,
I can finally write what i'm feeling.

I love it when I numb myself with weed,
I can finally remember your voice.

I love it when I numb myself with people,
I can finally forget how much I miss you.

I love it when I numb myself with your shows,
I can pretend we're watching together.

I love it when I numb myself with your music,
I can pretend we're singing together.

I love it when I numb myself with benadryl,
they put me to sleep only to wake me up
when you have time for me.

I love it when I numb myself.
I don't have to remember you're not here.

I love it when I numb myself.
I don't have to start the stages of grief.

I love it when I numb myself.
I don't have to accept, that we're out of time.

Seeds

"If I had an ass like yours, I would show it off"

"Look at that ass"

"You would be a pretty girl if you tried"

"You work so hard for your body, why don't you show it off"

"I created that ass, I get to touch it."

"Binging eating is all I gotta do to get a butt like yours? Damn, I should do it"

"Let me touch it, Let me touch it!"

"Take off your jacket and show off your body"

"Didn't you eat already"

"Don't think what you have here is love"

"You're too sensitive"

"You cry too much"

"You need to try not be so selfish"

"She's so selfish, and only cares for herself."

<3

winter reminds me of you.
because of the way
the morning breeze twinkles down my spine,
the same chills as I look into your eyes.
because in the most gorgeous winter sunset,
youre the better view.
because the moonlight was always pointing to you.
like the universe made that spotlight, just for you.
because we fell in love in the winter.
you were the warmth, the break,
that made everything better.

winter reminds me of you.
youve become my favorite season every year.
i mean, look at you...
how could you not be.

I don't want you to forget about me
and leave me behind.
We were supposed to heal together.
It's supposed to be you.
It's supposed to be you in the end.

My end.

<3

I still see you through my eyes, and every time I do. I smile, softly, innocently.

- I miss your soul

The one that got away:

and if this is the end of us.
come... revisit me.
in these pages,
where my love for you,
is everlasting.

-Thank you for making me fall in love with poetry again.
I love you.

Choose you.
Take yourself on dates.
Take yourself on long walks.
Learn your love language.
Learn all your layers.
Let yourself know, it's okay to let go. It's okay to cry and feel. It's okay to be vulnerable, I'm here. I'm listening to everything you're saying. I'm learning what you like, what you don't like. I'm learning every part, every form, every dimension, every constellation of you. I'm prioritizing you and your well-being.

I know our history and how inconsistent i've been, when it comes to loving and respecting you. But I wanna say, I'm sorry for putting others before you. This journey we are on together is the best decision i've ever made. I never knew how great, how wonderful, how beautiful you are as a person. How strong you are after everything that has tried to stop you. And I wished we would've started sooner, because loving you is the happiest i've ever been.

-fall for yourself

A passing note:

Be comfortable in your lonely.

A note to you:

I spent my youth craving attention from other people and abusing substances.
I numbed my family's pain and took advantage of their love to please these temporary people.

I spent my youth alone, hopping from girl to girl.
Afraid if i'm alone, I wasn't worth anything more than a regular person.
Allowing these temporary people to take me away from my family because of my need to be truly accepted.

Can I redeem myself for the pain I put you through,
because I can't go back and be there for the memories I missed.
Can you forgive me for the pain I put you through,
when I gave my life to the pills and you're there on my bedside praying, begging for me to stay.

I'm sorry for taking you for granted.
I was looking for love somewhere else and
only until now did I realize it was with you the entire time.
I'm trying to show you i'm worthy of your trust, your love.
That I am not going anywhere, but in your heart.

Do you have enough love for me
after everything I put you through?
Because i'm sorry and I know,
i'll forever have to redeem myself for the memories I missed.
I'll forever have to prove to you that I choose you,
over everything.

What did I do in a past life
to deserve someone like you.

-Karma

I fall too fast,
when someone tries to get my attention.

I fall too fast,
with the first person to ask questions about myself.

I fall too fast,
when someone shows me the bare minimum.

I fall too fast,
for it to be actually real.

A passing note:

You can't keep making the same excuses on staying here.

let me marinate in this growth a little while longer

A mother's love is where the word unconditional originates from.

<3

I never expected to fall in love.
But there's something about your soul,
that makes every part of me
intertwine into the person,
i've always dreamt to be.

-oh how heavenly

A passing note:

You don't need fixing,
You need healing.
There's a difference.

The feeling of knowing you're growing up.
That your youth is in the past.
That you're slowly fading out of your childhood problems.
Being scared that you wasted all of your childhood.
Longing to get it all back and
try again.

Outro:

I am the spitting image of my family's pain.
I am the lessons my siblings never learned.
I am the embodiment of everyone i've crossed paths with.

So thank you,
to everyone that I allowed,
to break me, to love me.
to anyone that was ever in my life.

Thank you for your time.

Sariaka's social media:

insta: sariakarazermera

twitter: SRazermera

tiktok: sariakaa

Printed in Great Britain
by Amazon